CHAPTER 4:
I DO NOT

THAT TV SHOW IS, LIKE, SO GOOD IT'S SCARY!
GOT THAT RIGHT!
WHERE'D I PUT MY HOMEWORK? I JUST KNOW I'M GOING TO BE CALLED ON TO GIVE AN ANSWER!

I HATED EVERYTHING ABOUT THE WORLD.

I'M SO WIPED! I JUST WANT THIS CLASS TO BE OVER!
I HEAR THERE'S THIS REALLY CUTE GUY IN SECOND YEAR! SMART AND ATHLETIC!
YOU'RE KIDDING! MAYBE I'LL TRY TO LAND A DATE!
YOU? HE'S OUT OF YOUR LEAGUE!

OR, RATHER, I JUST WASN'T INTERESTED.
THE VAPID CONVERSATIONS WHERE THE ONLY REPLY IS ALWAYS, "OH, IS THAT RIGHT?"
PLAYING THE "FRIENDS" GAME AND THE "LOVE" GAME LIKE A BUNCH OF IDIOTS.
YEAH.

IT'S ALL...

Story by MAGICA QUARTET • Art by MURA KUROE
PUELLA MAGI
ORIKO★MAGICA 2

PUELLA MAGI
ORIKO MAGICA
VOLUME TWO

WHICH WOULD BE AN INCIDENT THAT WOULD CHANGE HER DESTINY —
WHICH WOULD BE THE BEGINNING OF A WHOLE OTHER MAGICAL GIRL TALE —

PUELLA MAGI ORIKO☆MAGICA ❷

MAGICA QUARTET
MURA KUROE

Translation: William Flanagan • Lettering: Carl Vanstiphout

Yen Press
Hachette Book Group
237 Park Avenue, New York, NY 10017

www.HachetteBookGroup.com
www.YenPress.com

Yen Press is an imprint of Hachette Book Group, Inc. The Yen Press name and logo are trademarks of Hachette Book Group, Inc.

First Yen Press Edition: October 2013

ISBN: 978-0-316-25429-8

10 9 8 7 6 5 4 3 2 1

BVG

Printed in the United States of America

THANK YOU FOR COMING ALONG WITH US FOR THE WHOLE RIDE. I HOPE WE MEET AGAIN SOMETIME SOON.

MURA KUROE

...PATHETIC!

......

YOU KNOW, I'VE BEEN WAITING, LIKE, FOREVER!
TCH!
YOU'RE IN THE WAY. HURRY AND PICK THOSE UP!

CHARI (CLINK)
CHARIN

HYUA (VWWM)
DOSHU (FWOOM)
UNGH...

HYU (SLSH)
BA (SWOOP)
HIPA (FWAP)

YOU'RE THE FIRST MAGICAL GIRL WHO'S STAYED ALIVE THIS LONG!
A NEW RECORD! CONGRATU-LATIONS!
OH? IS THAT SO?
BUN (VOOM)
THEN I CAN'T WAIT TO BRAG ABOUT IT TO MY FRIENDS. I'M SURE IT WILL MAKE GREAT CONVERSATION AT TEA-TIME.
I'M IN TROUBLE.
MY MAGIC IS A BAD MATCH AGAINST HERS.
I HAVE THE POWER OF FIRE ON MY SIDE...
...BUT I HAVE TO SET UP MY SHOT BY AIMING AND PULLING THE TRIGGER FIRST.

SHE HAS THE SPEED TO GET OUT OF THE LINE OF FIRE IN THAT BRIEF MOMENT.

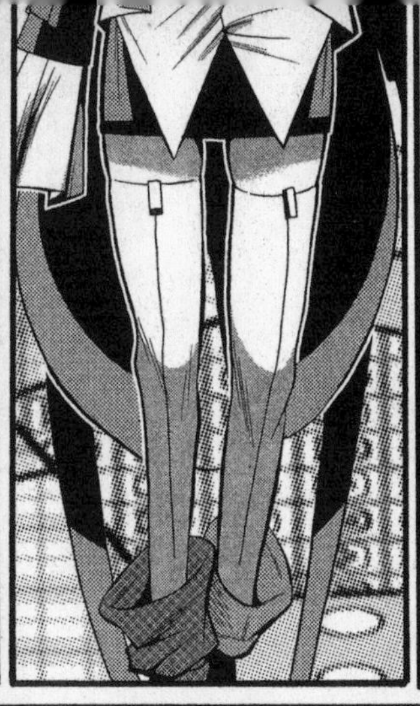

I ALSO SPECIALIZE IN BINDING MAGIC, BUT HER CUTTING WEAPONS RENDER THAT MAGIC...
...USE-LESS.

I'M BORED.
OH DEAR. YOU SEEM THE TYPE TO GET BORED EASILY...
...EVEN THOUGH NOTHING HAS BEEN SETTLED YET.
HOW VERY CHILDISH.
PIKU (TWITCH)

WHO...
...ARE YOU...
...CALLING...
BIKI (CRKL)

...A CH... CH...

...CHILD!?
DAHYU (VWSH)

GASHA (KACHAK)

YOU'RE TOO SLOW!
YOU'LL NEVER GET ME IN YOUR SIGHTS!
KA (TAK)
DOBANN (KABOOM)
!?

DO
(THNK)

SHUU
(WSHHH)

TCH...

USING YOUR GUN-SHOT AS A SMOKE-SCREEN TO RUN AWAY...?
I NEVER THOUGHT MY SAVIOR WOULD HAVE TO RESORT TO SNEAKY TACTICS.

YEAH...
BUT...
...STILL...
IT'S...
...NO...
...BIG DEAL.
PYON
(PYOING)

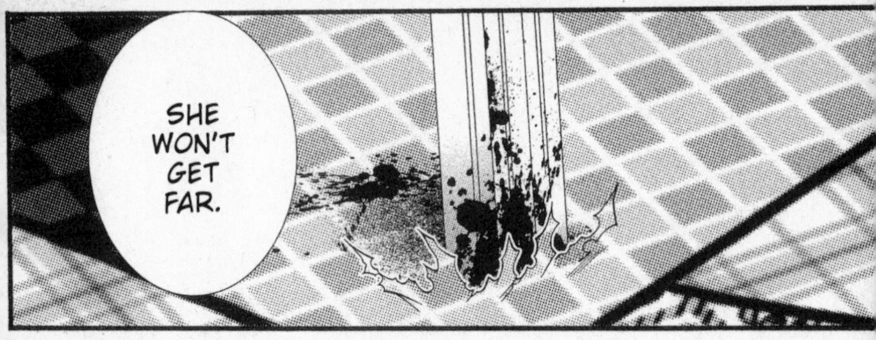
SHE WON'T GET FAR.

HAAH...
HAAH...

HAAH...
HAAH...
HAAH...

THIS IS BAD...I HAVE TO TREAT THIS QUICK!

WITH THIS WOUND, I WON'T BE ABLE TO EVEN DODGE HER ATTACKS, LET ALONE GO ON THE OFFENSIVE.

AND I CAN'T BRING DOWN THE WITCH'S WARDS AT THIS POINT EITHER...

ZUZUZUZUZU (THRUMMM)

I CAN'T GET AWAY...!

!

WHY?
THE WITCH IS DEAD, SO WHY IS IT TAKING SO LONG FOR THE WARDS TO COME DOWN?

SO THAT'S IT...! KIRIKA KURE ISN'T REALLY FAST AT ALL.
THAT GIRL'S MAGIC...

...SLOWS DOWN HER ENEMY...!

AND I FELL FOR IT...!

SHE DREW ME INTO THE WITCH'S WARDS ON PURPOSE.
BAN (BAM)
AND THAT'S WHEN SHE CAST THE SPELL...!

EVEN IF SHE'S MERELY SLOWING HER OPPONENTS DOWN, THE RESULT IS STILL THAT SHE'S INCREDIBLY FAST COMPARED TO ME.
WHAT WILL I DO?

I HAVE TO KEEP MOVING.
SHE'LL FIND ME HERE EVENTUALLY.

AND IT LOOKS LIKE I DON'T NEED TO CAST MY OWN MAGIC ON MY WOUND. THE BLEEDING HAS SLOWED ALREADY.

TEKE TEKE (TOTTER)

SLOWED...
THEN MAYBE...
BUO (VWOO)
ブォ
WILL THIS REALLY WORK ON HER...?
BASAA (FWISH)
I DON'T KNOW, BUT—
SCRATCH THAT!

パシッ
PASHI (GRIP)
I'LL MAKE IT WORK!
トッ
TO (TMP)

THIS IS BAD ...

THE WARDS ARE BEGINNING TO CRUMBLE.

I HAVE TO FINISH THIS!

ZUZUZUZUZU (RRRUMBLE)

....

IT'S NO BIG DEAL IF I LEAVE A MAGICAL GIRL'S CORPSE BEHIND, BUT IT'S AGAINST THE RULES TO LET ONE ESCAPE ALIVE.
I'LL BE FOUND OUT!

AND THAT WOULD LEAD TO ORIKO.
DA (LEAP)

I'M THE ONE WITH DIRTY HANDS.
ORIKO SHOULD JUST GIVE ORDERS.
I WILL NOT LET HER TAKE THE FALL ...!

NEVER!
I REFUSE TO GO BACK TO THE WAY I WAS!
バシャ
BASHA (CRASH)
JUST HURRY UP AND DO IT!
PEOPLE ARE WAITING! HURRY IT UP!
CHARI (CLINK)
CHARI
ちゃりちゃり

DO YOU THINK THAT'S ALL OF IT?

I'D HARDLY EVER BEEN TREATED WITH KIND-NESS BY SOMEBODY ELSE.
Y...
...YEAH.

BUT THAT WASN'T ALL.

THERE WAS SOMETHING ABOUT HER THAT DREW ME IN.
ONCE THEY'RE COOKED, I HAVE TO REMOVE THEM FROM THE MOLDS...
THEN WHAT WAS I SUPPOSED TO DO...?
JUUU (SIZZLE)
OWW!
HON-EST-LY!
WHY IS IT SO DIFFICULT TO MAKE SWEETS?
BUT IF I KNOW HER...
...SHE'S GOING TO COME RUSHING IN SCREAMING ABOUT HOW HUNGRY SHE IS.

HYUO (FWOOOO)
LOOK HOW SLOW YOU'RE MOVING!
SAVIOR, YOU MOVE LIKE A NEWBORN BABY.
I HOPE SHE GETS BACK SOON...
NOW I'VE GOT YOU!
IT'S TIME TO DO SOME CARVING!

DON (BOOM)
HYUPA (VWAPP)
KYAAA!
GO (WHAM)
DON (WHUD)
TAN (DASH)

WHAT'S THE PROBLEM? YOU COULD HAVE FINISHED ME OFF.
GOUN (VWWWM)

TA (TAP)

ZAZAA (SKIIID)

......
A BIG ONE, HUH...?
ZUZU (RMBL)
DON (DUNDUN)
YOU CERTAIN-LY ARE "FAST"...
...BUT YOUR ATTACKS LACK POWER.

SO BEFORE YOUR TEN CUTS CAN KILL ME...
...MY ONE SHOT WILL BRING YOU DOWN!
REALLY?
HEH HEH...
HEH!
HA!

IDIOT!

DO IT!

JUST GIVE IT A TRY!!

GASHA (VWSHH)

SHE HAS MORE TALONS NOW!!

IS THIS WHAT YOU WANT?
YOU ASKED FOR A WHOLE BUNCH OF ATTACKS, RIGHT?

TEN ATTACKS IN ONE, RIGHT?
NOW, PREPARE TO BE SLICED TO RIBBONS!

TA
(TMP)
I HAVE
ONLY
ONE
CHANCE!

DON
(BLAM)

SU (SSST)
NOW, BYE-BYE!
HYU (FYUU)
AW, YEAH!
NICE TRY, SAV-IOR!
GASHA (CRASH)

どしゃ
DOSHA
(WHUMP)

AH...
AHHH...
AH!
KIRIKA ...!
PAAN (BLAM)

FROM BEHIND ...?

H...

... HOW ...?

DON (BAM)

I GOADED YOU INTO PUTTING EVERYTHING YOU HAVE INTO A SINGLE ATTACK.
EVEN IF IT MEANT LIMITING YOUR SPEED-SLOWING MAGIC.
JUST BEHIND YOU, THERE WAS A BIT OF THE WITCH'S WARDS THAT WAS CRUMBLING FASTER THAN THE REST.
パキ…
......NH!
SO YOU LED ME INTO A TRAP!
BUT!
HOW DID YOU HIT ME IN THE BACK!?
I DIDN'T HIT YOU IN THE BACK.
WHAT I SHOT WAS AN EXPLODING BULLET.

NORMALLY IT'S A SHELL GUIDED BY MAGIC THAT IS SET TO EXPLODE IN FRONT OF THE ENEMY...
BUT YOUR MAGIC IS TO SLOW THE SPEED OF ANYTHING IN FRONT OF YOU.
YOU LET IT PASS YOU BY, BUT THE MOMENT IT WAS BEHIND YOU...

...IT WAS NO LONGER UNDER THE EFFECTS OF YOUR MAGIC, AND IT EXPLODED RIGHT ON YOUR BACK.
IN OTHER WORDS ...

...YOUR OWN MAGIC WAS YOUR DOWNFALL.

HA-HA-HA-HA-HA-HA-HA-HA-HA-HA-HA-HA-HA-HA...
YOU'RE GOOD, SAVIOR!

KEH-HEH-HEH-HEH! AH-HA-HA-HA-HA!
KIRIKA KURE...
THIS TIME I INSIST THAT YOU ANSWER MY QUESTIONS.
FORGET IT.

IF YOU DON'T BIND THOSE WOUNDS, YOU'LL DIE FROM BLOOD LOSS.

BA (WHOOSH)

YOU'LL GET NO AN-SWERS FROM ME!
I REFUSE TO ANSWER ANY-THING YOU COULD POS-SIBLY ASK OF ME!
FINE WITH ME!
SEE, I'M PREPARED TO DIE TO PROTECT WHAT I NEED TO!
SO I'M HAPPY TO DO IT!

TOO BAD.

GU (TUG)

GO- (WHOOM)

KYAAA-AAAA!
ドドドドッ
DODODODO (BABOOM)
WHA—!
WHAT JUST HAP-PENED?
AH!
ふわ
FUWA (LIFT)

A WHITE ...
... MAGICAL GIRL...
DO YOU HAVE ANY INFO ON A MAGICAL GIRL IN WHITE? SOMEBODY NAMED ORIKO.

I BELIEVE ...
...YOU HAVE HEARD OF ME.

ZUZUZUZU
(RRRUMBLE)

I IMAGINE YOU AND I SHALL MEET AGAIN.
AND AT THAT TIME...

...YOU WILL GET TO SEE HOW FOOLISH YOU'VE BEEN.
UNTIL THEN...
FU (FWFF)

DORO (DRIP)

I'VE NEVER FELT SO MUCH PRESSURE BEFORE...
SO THAT'S THE WHITE MAGICAL GIRL...

... ORIKO ...

I CAN'T STOP HER BLEED-ING...

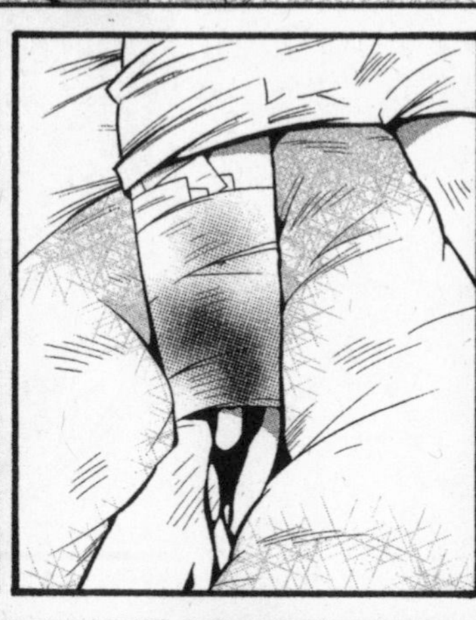

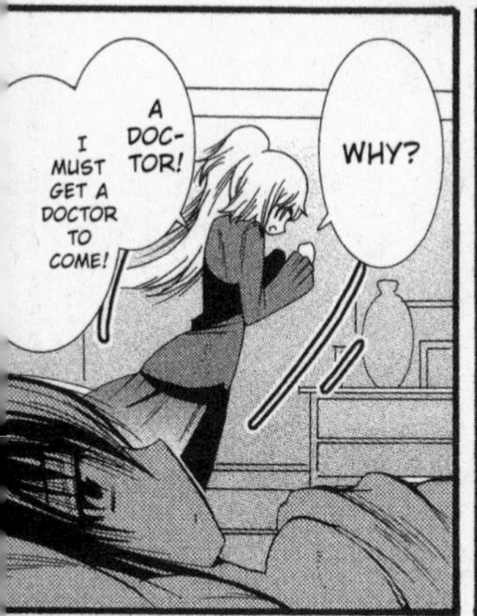
WHY?
A DOC-TOR! I MUST GET A DOCTOR TO COME!

SHE USED MY WEAK POINT AGAINST ME.
THAT MAMI TOMOE IS A GOOD FIGHTER.
ORIKO ...

I DON'T NEED A DOCTOR.
WHAT-EVER TREAT-MENT THEY HAVE, IT WON'T WORK ON THIS.

WH-WHAT ARE YOU SAYING?

IF WE DON'T DO SOMETHING, YOU'LL...

IT'S OKAY.

IT IS NOT!

FIRST THINGS FIRST.

I WANT YOU TO HEAR MY CONFESSION.

五郷駅
ITUSATO STASION
SIGN: TAXI STAND
←タクシー乗り場

IT WAS HER...
EVER SINCE THAT DAY, I SEARCHED THE TOWN FOR ORIKO.

I NEVER WENT TO SCHOOL MUCH ANYWAY, AND FROM THEN ON I HARDLY EVER SHOWED MY FACE THERE AGAIN. I NEVER EVEN THOUGHT MUCH ABOUT IT.

The train is entering the station. Please keep behind the...

I CAN JUST CALL OUT TO HER AND PRETEND IT'S A COINCI-DENCE.

WE'VE MET ONCE, SO...

...I'LL ASK IF...

I MEAN, WHO...
...WOULD EVER REMEMBER ME?
IT WAS A LIE WHEN I SAID THAT I WASN'T INTERESTED IN ANYTHING.
GOTO (KATNK)
PUSHUU (PSSHHH)
I WAS JUST PRETENDING TO BE DISINTERESTED.
GOTO
GOTO
PRETENDING TO LOOK DOWN ON EVERYBODY.
BUT I WAS JEALOUS.
THERE WAS NOBODY WHO WOULD GIVE ME...
...A SECOND THOUGHT.

I WANTED TO CHANGE...
I WANTED TO CHANGE INTO A DIFFERENT ME...
ぴょん
PYON (PYOING)
THAT WAS MY WISH.

I'M SORRY. THE GIRL YOU KNEW—THAT WAS A FAKE ME.

THE REAL ME IS SCARED TO DEATH OF BEING REJECTED.

I COULDN'T MAKE FRIENDS OR FIND SOMEONE TO LOVE ME. I COULDN'T EVEN FACE IT.

I WAS JUST A WEAK-WILLED CHILD.

ORIKO, I'M SORRY THAT I LED YOU ON WITH THAT LIE.
AND THANKS.

I DO NOT FORGIVE YOU.

I DO NOT FORGIVE YOU! I CAN'T!

YOU TRICKED ME, AND YOU HAVE THE DUTY TO ATONE FOR THAT CRIME.

YOU ARE TO PROTECT ME *NO MATTER WHAT THAT MAY DO TO YOU.*

I WILL NOT FORGIVE ANYTHING LESS.

RIGHT.
IT'S A PROMISE.
HAAH...
IT'S OVER! IT'S FINALLY OVER!

...MADOKA.

BOY, AM I HUNGRY!
LET'S STOP SOMEPLACE AND EAT.
HEY, GOOD IDEA!
ICE CREAM SOUNDS GOOD! I COULD DOWN A TRIPLE!
SAYAKA-SAN, YOU'LL GET A STOMACHACHE.

I THINK I'D PREFER DONUTS.
HOW ABOUT YOU, HOMURA-CHAN?

I WANT TO EAT WHATEVER YOU WANT...

PUELLA MAGI

ORIKO☆MAGICA

HEY, IT'S HER! PRESIDENT OF THE STUDENT COUNCIL AND TOP IN HER CLASS...
ORIKO MIKUNI-SAN.
SIMPLY LOVELY! HIGH TEA WITH HER WOULD CERTAINLY BE A TREAT!
EVERYBODY IN OUR SCHOOL IS SO PROUD OF PRESIDENT MIKUNI!
WELL, THAT'S OUR CHARMING YOUNG MISS MIKUNI FOR YOU.
A VERY BRIGHT YOUNG LADY.
I HOPE SHE DOES HER BEST NOT TO DO ANYTHING THAT MIGHT EMBARRASS HER FATHER.

Today, National Diet Representative Hisaomi Mikuni was found hanged by the neck in his home.

He was transported to the hospital and pronounced dead at 2:00 p.m. today.

The police have been investigating allegations of falsified expense reports, and sources speculate there is a high probability that his death was a suicide to avoid police questioning.

It is time for morning announce-ments.
Will all students please return to your class-rooms.
KYUBEY, YOU KNEW WHO WAS HUNTING MAGICAL GIRLS ALL ALONG, DIDN'T YOU?
I HAD SUSPI-CIONS.
BUT HOW COULD I GO ACCUSING HER WITHOUT ANY PROOF?
......
I'LL ALLOW YOU TO GET AWAY WITH THAT ANSWER...
...BUT MORE IM-POR-TANT-LY...
...WHY WOULD THOSE GIRLS WANT TO DO THAT?
OOOOOO
ORIKO IS...
This morn-ing—
EEEEK!!

GO (SLAM)
...USING HER MAGICAL GIRL POWERS...
OH DEAR! YOU KNOW IT'S WRONG TO USE VIOLENCE AGAINST A TEACHER.
DON'T WORRY ABOUT IT!
ORIKO AND I...
...HAVE NOW TAKEN CONTROL...
...OF THIS BROAD-CAST!
...TO TRY TO TAKE POSSES-SION OF THE WORLD, IN MY ESTI-MATION.
CHAPTER 5: THAT IS WHY I AM HERE

WHA ...!?
EH? WHAT? WHAT HAPPENED TO THE ANNOUNCEMENTS?
IT'S JUST THE DRAMA CLUB HAVING A BIT OF FUN, RIGHT?
THE GIRL WITH LONG HAIR IS REALLY PRETTY, HUH?
ZAWA
ZAWA
ZAWA (CHATTER)
Testing, testing. One, two, three...
Kirika, you're not facing the camera.
EH?
WHAT? WHAT'S GOING ON?
WHO ARE THOSE GUYS?
IT'S ALL RIGHT. THERE IS NOTHING TO WORRY ABOUT.
HOMURA-CHAN ...

YOU'RE PLANNING THE FINAL SHOWDOWN, ORIKO...?
I'VE FIGURED OUT YOUR POWER.
AND YOUR OBJEC-TIVE.
ORIKO MIKUNI.
I WILL SEE YOU ELIMI-NATED.
IT'S OUT-RA-GEOUS.
I CAN NEVER UNDERSTAND WHAT YOU... WHAT YOU HUMANS ARE THINKING!

ZAWA (CHATTER)
ZAWA
HEY, ISN'T THAT A SHIROME UNIFORM?
WHAT WOULD A PRINCESS FROM A FANCY GIRL'S SCHOOL BE DOING HERE?
ORIKO MIKUNI...!
WHY WOULD YOU WANT TO DRAW ATTENTION TO YOURSELF LIKE THIS?
I wonder if each you...
...has some-one...
...that you love.

Your family, a lover, a good friend ...
People you love with all your heart. People you'd risk your life for.
And when you find you cannot protect them, have you ever felt misery at your own power-lessness?
THE WORLD IS BESET WITH GREAT DANGER.
PURE EVIL AND VIOLENCE DOES EXIST.
IT HAS TAKEN FORM AND IS TRYING TO COME HERE.
HUH?
WHAT IS THAT GIRL TALKING ABOUT? IS SHE RIGHT IN THE HEAD?
SHE SEEMS LIKE AN ODD ONE, ALL RIGHT.
EVERY-ONE, PLEASE BE QUIET.
THE TEACHERS WILL GO TO THE P.A. ROOM TO ASSESS THE SITU-ATION, SO JUST STAY SEATED.

BUT...
...I WILL FIGHT IT!

DID SHE... JUST SEE ME?

ZOKU (SHIVER)
!?

COME IF YOU WISH, YOU DEEPEST OF TRAGEDIES.

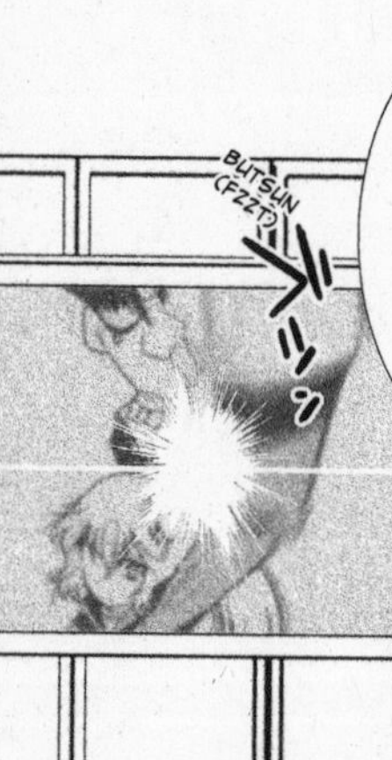
BUTSUN (FZZT)

SO... WHAT WAS THAT ALL ABOUT ANY-WAY?
I DON'T GET IT.

!!
ZU
(ZIMM)
PAAAAAAN
(CRAAAAAASH)
KYAA-
AAAA
!!

DON (SLAM)
EHH ...?
WHAT IS THIS?
DON
DON
THE CLASSROOM IS CHANGING!
NO! THIS IS SCARY!
SAYAKA-CHAN, I DON'T LIKE THE FEELING I'M GETTING HERE!
ME NEITHER!

E-EVERYONE, JUST KEEP CALM—

HUH ...?
UM, IS THERE SOMETHING ON MY SHOUL-DER?

GOKIN (GRUNCH)

GOKI (GRUNCH)
GOKI
GOKI
GOKI

KARAN (ROLL)

WAAAAAH!
OW! OW! OW!
HEY, YOU GUYS, WHERE ARE YOU?
KYAA!
MADOKA!
OWW ...
HONESTLY... PUSHING ME BACK WHILE YOU RUN PAST! THAT'S JUST AWFUL!

!!
NO WAY...
SOMEBODY!
SOMEBODY HELP ME!
I'M SCARED! MAKE IT STOP!
AHHH! GROSS! GET AWAY FROM ME!
GO AWAY, YOU LITTLE—
QUIT PUSHING!
HURRY UP, IDIOT!
WHAT ARE THE TEACHERS EVEN DOING?
I CAN HEAR SOMEBODY SCREAMING! WAS SOMEBODY ATTACKED?
HOW SHOULD I KNOW!? WE JUST HAVE TO GET OUT OF HERE!
I DON'T THINK... I CAN LAST MUCH—
BABAN (BA-BAM)

BESHA (SPLAT)
AND ANYBODY WHO GETS IN THE WAY...
...!?
...LOTS OF INTER-ESTING THINGS IN HERE, HUH?
...WILL BE DEALT WITH!
WELL, WHAT-EVER.
KO (TAK)
KO
I REALLY ONLY HAVE ONE TASK WHEREVER I AM.
KO

DON (BLAM)
BASHI (BLATCH)
GA GSH
GET BACK!

THERE'S NO END TO THEM!

IT'S IMPOSSIBLE TO RES-CUE THE STUDENTS ONE AT A TIME.

I HAVE TO BRING DOWN THIS WITCH—AND FAST!

!?

A WITCH'S CURSE?
NO... THERE'S A DEFINITE WILL AT WORK HERE.

DOKYA (DO-CHOOM)

SO THAT'S THE DEEP-EST POINT ...

VUN (VWSH)

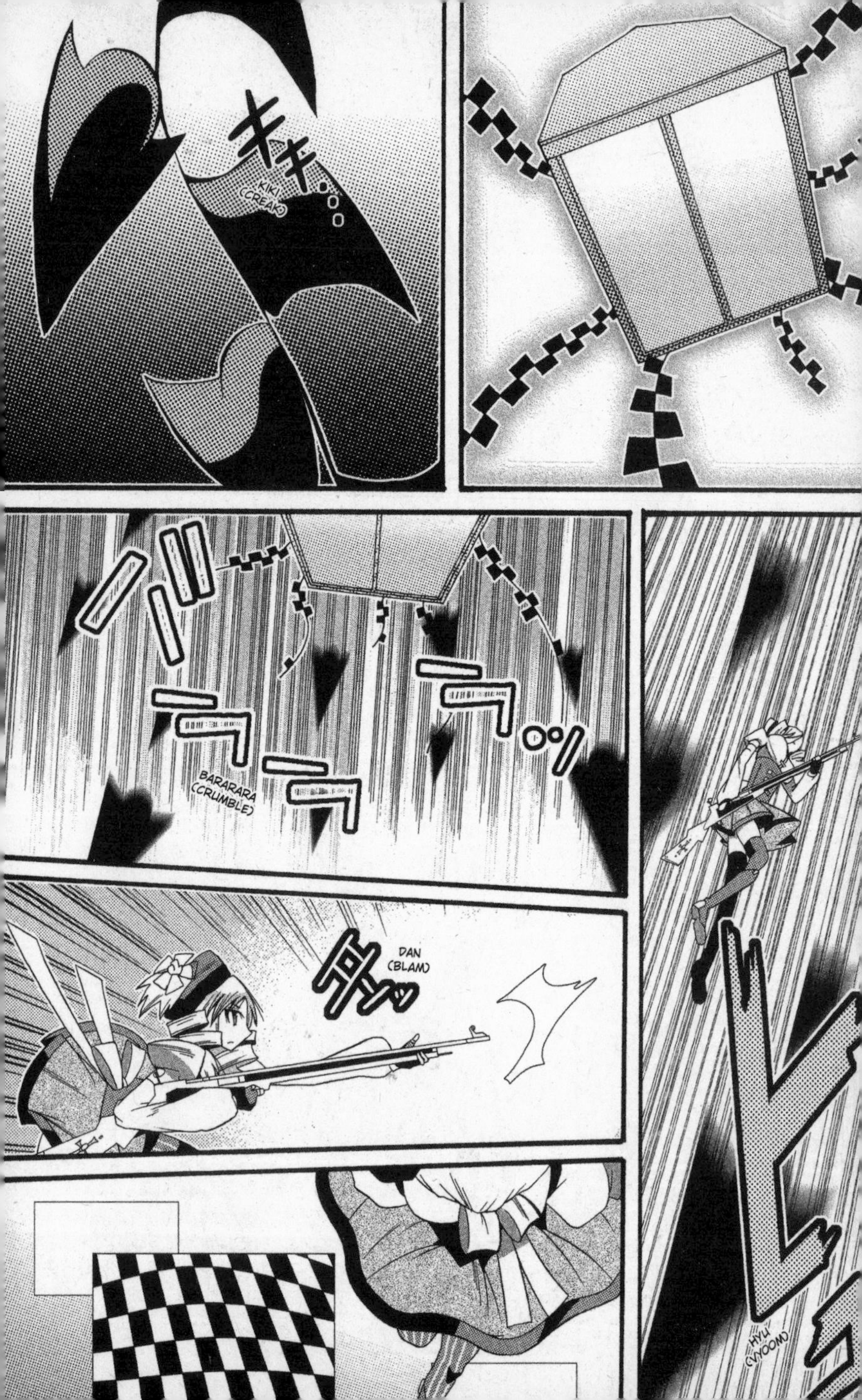
KIKI (CREAK)
BARARARA (CRUMBLE)
DAN (BLAM)
HYU (VYOOM)

HYUN
BASHI (GRAB)

OH NO!
IT CAME AT ME FROM UNDER-NEATH!

MMN ...
MM-MH ... NH ...!

OH NO. NOW SHE'S BEEN CAUGHT.
AW, GEEZ!
WHAT DOES SHE THINK SHE'S DOING?

HYUPA (SLASH)
YOU TWO... WHAT ARE YOU DOING HERE?
3F
ARE YOU HURT? I CAN FIX IT!
I'M ONLY HERE BECAUSE KYUBEY CALLED ME HERE. HE SAID THE WHITE MAGICAL GIRL WAS ON SOME KINDA RAMPAGE.

I CAN'T SAY I BUY HIS LINE...
...BUT I GOT A SCORE TO SETTLE WITH ORIKO.
I SEE... BUT...
ARE YOU SURE THIS IS A GOOD PLACE TO BRING SUCH A YOUNG GIRL?
EH?
I CAN FIGHT AS GOOD AS ANYBODY!
I CAN HELP!
HEH HEH... THEN I'LL EXPECT GREAT THINGS FROM YOU. DO YOUR BEST.
HEE HEE!
GRR! YOU DON'T TRUST ME AT ALL, DO YOU?
HEY! CUT THE CHIT-CHAT!
I'M GOIN' IN THERE!

HOMURA-CHAN!

DOGON (DWHAM)

HO-MURA-CHAN!

TAN (TMP)

TAN

HO-MURA-CHAN!!

NO...

THAT'S WRONG...
THAT'S NOT HOW IT SHOULD BE!

WHY NOT?

WHY ARE YOU...
...PROTECTING ONLY ME?

MA-DO-KA?

I'M REALLY HAPPY THAT YOU CAME TO SAVE ME...
...BUT... BUT...

...BUT SAYAKA-CHAN AND HITOMI-CHAN ARE HERE TOO!
WARA (CROWD)
WARA
THAT'S AWFUL...
BOTH OF THEM ARE OUR FRIENDS TOO!
WARA
GAFU (GULP)

HOW CAN YOU ACT SO CALM ABOUT ALL THIS?

WHY?
WHY AM I THE ONLY ONE YOU'RE SAVING?
YOU'VE GOT SO MUCH POWER, HO-MURA-CHAN!!

IF YOU PLAN TO LET ALL THE OTHERS DIE...
...THEN IT'D BE BETTER IF YOU DIDN'T SAVE ME...!
MADOKA ...
...DON'T EVER TELL ME NOT TO SAVE YOU.

I'M NOT ALL-POWERFUL.
I AM NOT ABLE TO SAVE EVERYONE.
BUT...
...EVEN SO, I WANT TO SAVE YOU.

SO DON'T SAY THAT ANYMORE!

WHA—?
FON (FWOOM)

I'LL GO ON ALONE FROM HERE.
AS LONG AS YOU'RE IN THIS WARD I'VE SET, THE FAMILIARS WON'T ATTACK YOU.
DON'T MOVE FROM THAT SPOT UNTIL I GET BACK.

HOMURA-CHA—
OW!
PACHI (VZZT)
HO-MURA-CHAN...
...I SAID SOME AWFUL THINGS TO YOU. I'M SORRY.
LET'S ...
LET'S GO HOME TOGETHER ...

KA (TAK)
KA
DON (BOOM)
THAT IS WHY I AM HERE.
TO MAKE SURE YOU COME BACK ...

WEL-
COME.

KA
(TAK)

ZU
(ZLIMM)

TAKE DOWN THESE WITCH'S WARDS.

YOU'RE THE ONES WHO PUT THEM UP IN THE FIRST PLACE, RIGHT?

WHATEVER ARE YOU TALKING ABOUT?

......

!!

BAM (BLAM)

WELL, AREN'T YOU A SCARY ONE?
I SUPPOSE YOU NEVER INTENDED TO TALK IN THE FIRST PLACE.
DOKAKA (KACHOOM)
!?
IT DIDN'T HIT THEM?
I KNOW ALL ABOUT YOU.
YOU WERE THERE.

AT THE END OF THE WORLD.

I HAVE...
...SEEN IT OVER AND OVER AGAIN.
IT'S FAST AP-PROACH-ING.
AND I'VE BEEN SEARCH-ING FOR A WAY TO SAVE THE WORLD.

ALSO, I KNOW WHAT THE THING ACTUALLY IS.

...IS THAT...

...ANY KIND OF REASON FOR PUTTING UP WITCH'S WARDS AT THE SCHOOL?

I'M SURPRISED.

KA (FLASH)

YOU ARE THE SAME *"YOU"* WHO *WAS IN THAT PLACE*, ARE YOU NOT?

IF YOU WERE...

...THEN YOU SHOULD UNDERSTAND WHAT I AM TALKING ABOUT.

I WISH TO AVOID THAT END...

...AND SAVE THE WORLD.

MADOKA KANAME MUST BE ELIMINATED.

GAHYU (KAYOOM)

GA (GSH)

GA

GA

YOU'VE SEEN IT YOUR-SELF, AND STILL YOU WILL NOT SURREN-DER MADOKA KANAME?

HOW REGRET-TABLE.

ZASHI (SLASH)

SHE'S FAST!

BUN (FOOM)

GOGOGON (GOWHOOM)

!

YOU THINK I'D FALL FOR THE *SAME TRICK* TWICE!?

OH MY.
WE HAVE MORE GUESTS.
PER-HAPS YOU THREE WILL HEAR ME OUT.

NOW ISN'T THAT ODD? THERE IS NO WITCH TO BE SEEN.

WHO CARES? ONCE WE TAKE DOWN ORIKO, IT'S ALL OVER, RIGHT?

ORO (PANIC) ORO

IT WON'T BE THAT EASY.

FIRST WE HAVE TO DO SOMETHING ABOUT THESE WARDS.

...SO WHAT IS THIS? YOU THINK NOW YOU CAN SHED A FEW TEARS, SAY YOU'RE SORRY, AND GET OFF EASY?

......

YOU POOR THINGS.

FOUR AGAINST... NO.
I WASN'T EVEN ABLE TO DEFEAT MAMI TOMOE ALONE. I'LL JUST BE IN YOUR WAY...
...AS LONG AS I'M A MAGICAL GIRL.

?

!
KIRIKA!
IT'S ABOUT TIME FOR IT, ORIKO.

AS I AM NOW...
...I'M JUST *CLOSE ENOUGH* THAT I CAN ALREADY PUT UP WARDS.

...AH!
IT'S ALL RIGHT! NO MATTER WHAT I TURN INTO, I WOULD NEVER HURT YOU, ORIKO!
I NEVER GUESSED... THE ONE WHO PUT UP THESE WARDS WAS...
THIS IS BETTER. IF I CAN PROTECT YOU BY BECOMING THIS...
...THEN I...
WHAT?
WHOA!
...GLADLY SURRENDER TO DESPAIR!
BUAAA (VWAAA)

KI-RIKA...
...IT WILL NOT BE YOU WHO TRULY DESPAIRS.
THE TRUE DESPAIR WILL FALL UPON THOSE GIRLS!
ZUZU (ZWOOM)

GRAFFITI: GET OUT! TAX THIEF! DIE!
BE-TRAYED.
BY MY OWN FATHER.
CHAPTER 6: SOMEDAY IS NOT NOW
HEH-HEH! HOW DARE SHE SHOW HER FACE AT SCHOOL!?
SOME NERVE! SHE'S BRINGING DOWN OUR SCHOOL'S REPUTATION BY JUST BEING HERE!
SOMEONE WITH A THIEF'S GENES SHOULDN'T BE SO UPPITY!
HEH HEH HEH HEH!
BY EVERY-THING.
NO, HE WILL NOT SEE YOU.
AND I THINK YOU WOULD DO WELL TO UNDERSTAND YOUR POSITION RIGHT NOW.
IT CERTAINLY WOULDN'T DO TO BE SEEN WITH THE DAUGHTER OF A CROOKED REPRESENTA-TIVE SO CLOSE TO ELECTIONS, RIGHT?
BY EVERY-ONE I TRUSTED ...

YOU HAVE TALENT.
TAKE UP THE CALLING TO FIGHT AGAINST WITCHES...
THAT IS, IF YOU WANT YOUR FUTURE TO OPEN UP TO YOU.
WHO...
...WHO ARE YOU?
YOU'D DO WELL TO CONTRACT WITH ME.

ZASHA (SLASH)
KIRIKA KURE
1996-2011 DEAD
VUN (VWM)
THE MAGI-CAL GIRL...
...TURNED INTO...
...A WITCH!?

HYAH!

GA (CRASH)

GO (VWOOM)

GURA (WOBBLE)

THIS COULD WORK!

DON (BLAM)

WAAAAH!?
MAMI, WHAT'RE YOU DOING? DON'T GET IN MY WAY!
YOU'RE THE ONE WHO SHOULD WATCH WHERE YOU'RE LEAPING IN! QUIT GETTING IN MY LINE OF SIGHT!

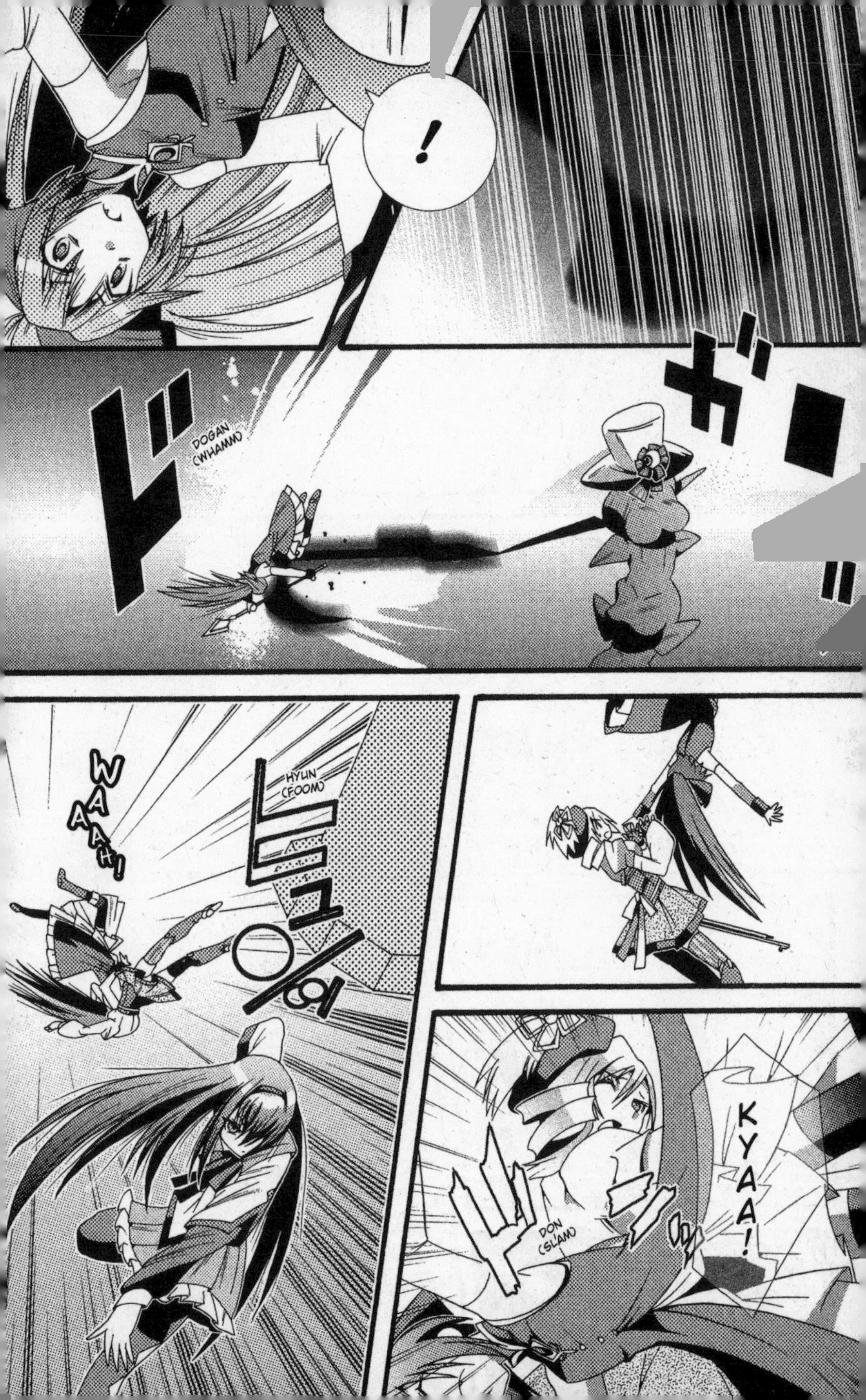
!
DOGAN (WHAMM)
HYUN (FOOM)
WAAAH!
KYAAA!
DON (SLAM)

HYU
(WHOOSH)
WHA—!?
KACHIN
(KACHIK)
IT'S FAST...
WE'RE AT A DISADVANTAGE IN A PROLONGED FIGHT.
!
GASHI
(GRAB)
KACHI
(CLICK)

DOKAAA (BLAAAM)

POI (FLOP)

OWW!

I'LL TAKE THEM.

YOU ALL ARE JUST IN MY WAY.
STAY OUT OF IT.

WHA—!? DON'T GIVE ME THAT CRAP!

I SEE THAT NONE OF YOU ARE WILLING TO ACCEPT THE TRUTH.

YET THEY REFUSE TO ACCEPT IT.
THEY TREAT IT AS ALIEN. AS POISON.
THEY TRY TO VOMIT IT OUT, BUT IT HAS SUNK IN AND BEGINS TO BREAK THEM.
AND SO...

THOSE GIRLS SHOULD BE ABLE TO UNDER-STAND WHAT HAS HAP-PENED.

...WITH THEIR HEARTS IN CHAOS, THEY CANNOT FIGHT AS THEY SHOULD.

JUST LIKE THOSE OTHER MAGICAL GIRLS...

I PITY THESE MAGICAL GIRLS.
THESE GIRLS REFUSE TO UNDERSTAND THEIR TRUE FATE, SO THEY SIMPLY STAND AND FIGHT.
I KNOW THE FACE OF REAL HORROR.
SO THIS TRUTH HOLDS NO FEAR FOR ME.
SO AT LEAST I WILL GRANT THEM A SPEEDY DEATH!
DO
DO
DO
DO (BAM)

THAT'S RIGHT.

YOU KNEW IT TOO.

DO DO DO

WE COULD HAVE BEEN A GOOD TEAM, BUT...

...THAT WON'T HAPPEN NOW, WILL IT?

YOU ATTEMPT TO PROTECT MADOKA KANAME!

YOU'RE TRYING TO KILL MADOKA!

UU...
UWAAAAAH!

YOU LITTLE... DIE! DIE!
POKAN (POK)

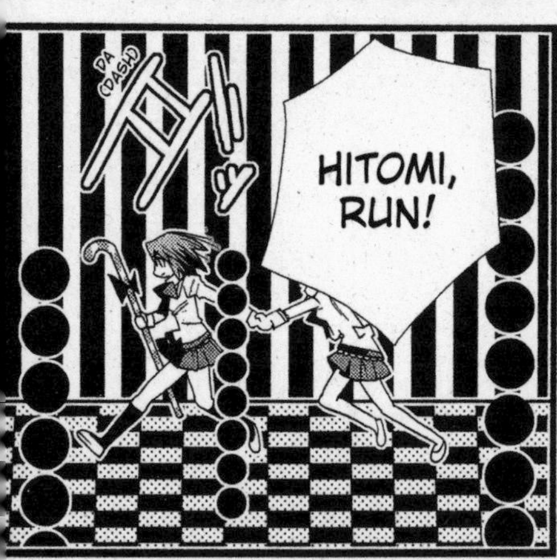
DA (DASH)
HITOMI, RUN!

SA-YAKA-SAN, WHAT ARE THESE THINGS?
I DON'T KNOW!

I DON'T KNOW WHERE WE ARE OR WHERE THE EXIT IS! NOT A CLUE!
TA (TMP)
TA
TA
TA
I WISH SOMEBODY'D TELL ME!

BIKU (TWITCH)
BIKU

!

I CAN'T TAKE THIS ANY-MORE!

HITOMI, YOU CAN'T STOP HERE!
I DON'T CARE ANYMORE! I'D RATHER DIE THAN GO THROUGH ANY MORE OF THIS...

S-STOP THAT! GET AWAY...
GET AWAY FROM ME!
KACHI (CLICK)

ELEVATOR
1-3F
POKON
(POP)

A MAGICAL GIRL TURNED INTO A WITCH!?

DOES THAT MEAN I'M GOING TO TURN INTO THAT TOO?

AHHH!
GA (GSH)
DON'T GET CARRIED AWAY!
HIPA (SLIP)
DAM-MIT—
GOKYA (KRABAM)
WAAH!

KYOUKO ...?
MAMI-ONEECHAN ...?

I SEE NOW. YOUR MAGIC CONTROLS TIME.
KYUN (SHUUM)
NOW I UNDERSTAND YOUR EXISTENCE HERE.

MY GUESS IS ORIKO MIKUNI'S MAGIC IS FORESIGHT.
BUT SHE COULDN'T AVOID MY ATTACKS WITH JUST THAT.

THAT WITCH'S SPEED MUST BE INFLUENCING HER AS WELL.
SHE READS THE ATTACK WITH HER FORESIGHT AND USES HIGH SPEED TO AVOID THE BULLETS BEFORE THEY HIT.
I KNOW THAT I SHOULD BE TAKING OUT THAT WITCH FIRST, BUT...

...SHE PROBABLY ALREADY KNOWS THAT TOO... HUH...?

BA (WHOOSH)
BUN (FWOOM)
WHY DOES THIS DIMENSION HAVE SO MANY IRREGULARITIES ...?
HOW MANY TIMES HAVE YOU REPEATED THIS?
AND HOW MANY TIMES DO YOU INTEND TO REPEAT IT AFTER THIS?

ALL THOSE DARK PATHS YOU HAVE WALKED ...
...DID YOU FIND ANYTHING CLOSE TO WHAT YOU WERE SEARCHING FOR?
STOP TALK-ING...
SHUT UP!
I AM DIFFERENT FROM YOU.
HYU! (SHUP)

ZA
(SHKK)
WHEN THE ROAD IS DARK, I BRING OUT MY OWN LIGHT.
YOU KEEP RUNNING AWAY TO DIFFERENT PATHS...
...SO THERE IS NO WAY YOU COULD DEFEAT ME!
DOKYA
(THWACK)

DABA (SPURT)
DO- (WHUD)

AH...
AHH...

HOLD ON! I'LL FIX YOU UP!

DON'T...! YUMA, JUST RUN AWAY!

EH?
SHE'S RIGHT... WHAT'S THE POINT OF HEALING OUR WOUNDS?
YOU SAW IT, DIDN'T YOU? WITCHES ARE BORN FROM OUR SOUL GEMS.

...

IF I'M GOING TO END UP AS A WITCH. THEN I WOULD RATHER SIMPLY DIE RIGHT HERE...

GOGOGO (RUMBLE)

IT SEEMS OUR FIGHT IS OVER.

BUO (VWOO)

DOBAN (FWOOSH)

!
PAA (GLOW)

I'M CURED.
YUMA !?
YOU KNOW I... USED TO THINK THAT EVERY TIME MY MAMA PICKED ON ME...
...THAT I'D RATHER BE DEAD.

BUT WHEN THAT WITCH ATTACKED US AND I THOUGHT I WAS GOING TO DIE...
...I DID EVERYTHING I COULD TO STAY ALIVE.

SOME-DAY WE'LL PROB-ABLY BE-COME WITCH-ES!

BUT SOMEDAY IS NOT NOW!

EVERY-BODY'S GOING TO DIE SOMEDAY.

SO ARE YOU, KYOUKO... AND YOU, MAMI-ONEECHAN...
...REALLY GOING TO DIE RIGHT NOW?
GUSHA (CRUNCH)

KKH...

AM I...
...GOING TO FAIL AGAIN...?
SHUUU (PSHHH)

DO I REALLY NOT STAND A CHANCE EVEN AGAINST THESE TWO?

AM I...

...GOING TO LOSE HER AGAIN?

GAN (CRACK)

DOGA
(BOOM)
GA
GA
GA
GA

...!
WHA—!?
KIRIKA!?
MAMI TOMOE'S RAPID FIRE...
THEN YUMA USES HER ATTACK WAVE TO ALTER THE BULLETS' PATH...
...MAKING THEM NEARLY IMPOSSIBLE TO AVOID.
DARTING BETWEEN VOLLEYS LIKE THREADING A NEEDLE THROUGH THE HAIL OF BULLETS, KYOUKO SAKURA UNLEASHES HER OWN ATTACKS.

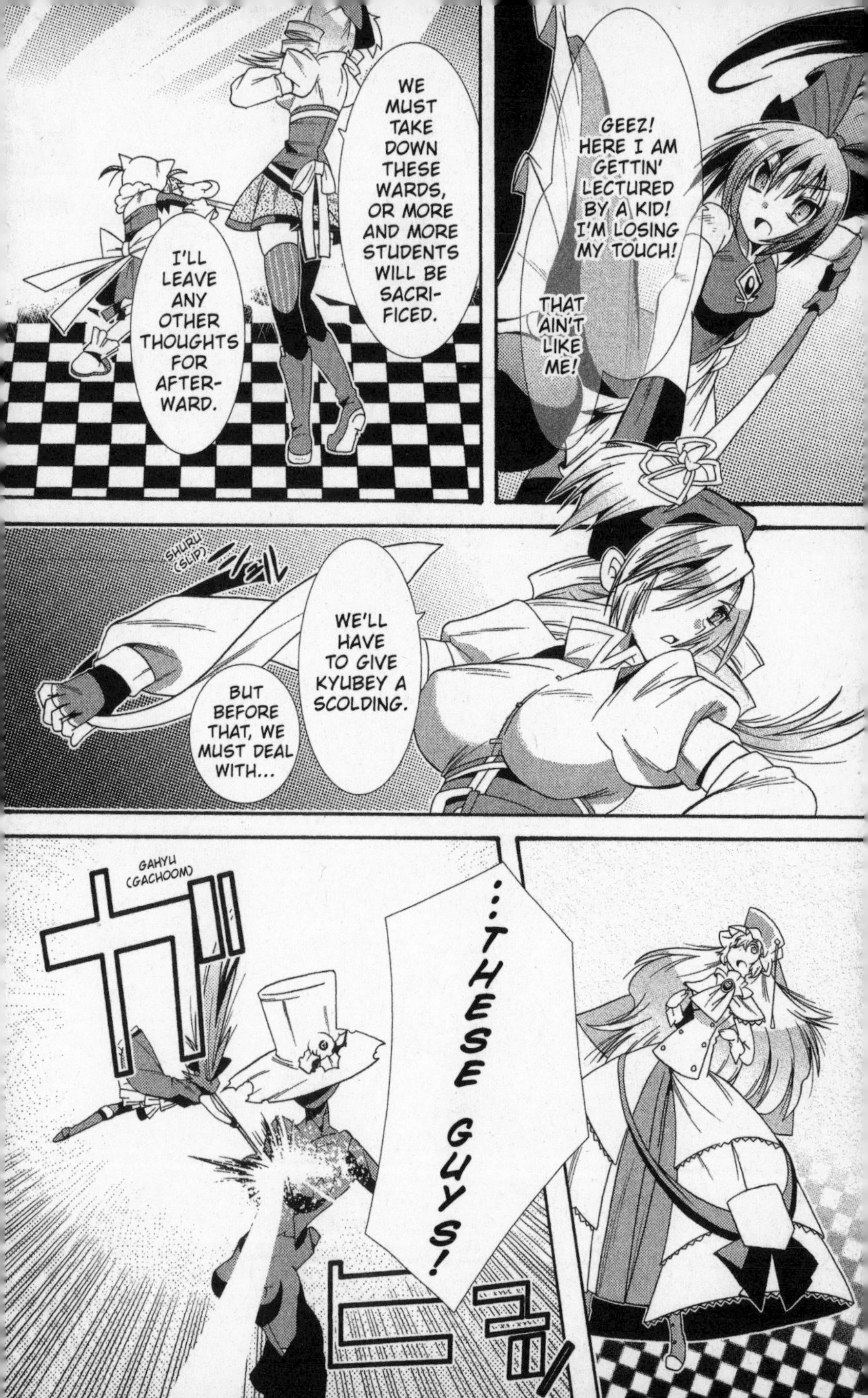
GEEZ! HERE I AM GETTIN' LECTURED BY A KID! I'M LOSING MY TOUCH!
THAT AIN'T LIKE ME!
WE MUST TAKE DOWN THESE WARDS, OR MORE AND MORE STUDENTS WILL BE SACRI-FICED.
I'LL LEAVE ANY OTHER THOUGHTS FOR AFTER-WARD.
SHURU (SLIP)
WE'LL HAVE TO GIVE KYUBEY A SCOLDING.
BUT BEFORE THAT, WE MUST DEAL WITH...
...THESE GUYS!
GAHYU (GACHOOM)

TIRO...
...FINALE!
DOPAAN (BLAAAM)
ZAZAZAZA (SKIIIIID)
KIRIKA!
DA (DASH)

KA (TAK)
WHERE DO YOU THINK YOU'RE GOING?
DON (BLAM)
CHI (SNIP)
HOMURA AKEMI...
...GET BACK!
DAKYU (DWOOM)

WHY...
...DO YOU GIRLS ...
...AL-WAYS ...
...GET IN OUR WAY!?

IF YOU KEEP USING YOUR MAGIC LIKE THAT, YOU'LL BECOME A WITCH AS WELL.

YOU DON'T KNOW WHEN TO GIVE UP, DO YOU? SURRENDER NOW!
ZA (SHK)

THERE IS NOTHING LEFT FOR YOU.
WE AREN'T GOING TO DO ANYTHING BAD TO YOU.

IT'S OVER, ORIKO MIKUNI.

THESE GIRLS WERE FULL OF DESPAIR, UNABLE TO ACCEPT THEIR FATES.

BUT NOW...
...THEY ARE UNITED.

COULD IT BE THAT THIS HIGHLY IRREGU-LAR DIMEN-SION...

...IS THE ONE WHERE I WILL FIND THE MIRACLE THAT WILL ALLOW MY JOURNEYS TO END...?

—TASHI (THUMP)

YOU REALLY ARE A PROBLEM CHILD, AREN'T YOU, ORIKO?

IT WAS ALL TO TAKE MY EYE OFF OF THAT GIRL.

THAT'S WHY YOU TOLD ME ABOUT YUMA AND STARTED THIS WHOLE RUCKUS ABOUT A MAGICAL GIRL HUNTER, RIGHT?
THEN YOU CREATED THIS CONFUSION ALL TO FINISH HER OFF BEFORE I COULD MAKE HER A MAGICAL GIRL.
BUT SHE HAD A PROTECTOR YOU WEREN'T EXPECTING.
AND THAT RESULTED IN THIS DESPERATE ATTACK.

WHAT A SHAME, HUH?
INCUBATOR...!!
WELL, I FOUND HER.
BACHI (VZZT)
URRRH... AHHHHH!

PAAAN (BLAM)
GOCHIIIN (WHUD)
EVEN IF I GO...
Ow! Ow! Ow!
...I DON'T KNOW IF I CAN BE OF ANY HELP, BUT...
TO (WOBBLE)
...I CAN'T JUST LEAVE HER ALONE!
I'VE FOUND MADOKA KANAME.

PUELLA MAGI

ORIKO ★ MAGICA

FINAL CHAPTER: TO PROTECT MY WORLD

MIKUNI-SAN SEEMS TO BE ABLE TO DO JUST ABOUT ANYTHING.
WHEN YOU'RE FROM SUCH A GOOD FAMILY, THAT'S JUST PAR FOR THE COURSE.

MIKUNI-SENPAI, YOU'RE AMAZING!
THAT'S REPRESENTATIVE MIKUNI'S DAUGHTER FOR YOU. BEAUTY AND CLASS!
MIKUNI-SAN.

THE DAUGHTER OF REPRESENTATIVE MIKUNI.
SUCH A PRIM YOUNG LADY WOULD WANT FOR NOTHING.
A PERFECT HUMAN BEING WHO SUCCEEDS AT EVERYTHING.
HER ACHIEVEMENTS ARE ONLY NATURAL.
AFTER ALL, SHE'S A MIKUNI.

ORIKO!

SAYAKA-CHAN! HITOMI-CHAN, ARE YOU TWO ALL RIGHT?

HAAH...

HAAH...

I WAS JUST A HAIR FROM DEATH!

THANK GOODNESS WE FOUND A PLACE WITHOUT THOSE MONSTERS!

AND AS A BONUS, MADOKA'S HERE TOO! HOW'D WE GET SO LUCKY? HA-HA!

SAYAKA-CHAN, HOW ARE THINGS DOWN BELOW?

I HAVE TO GO...

GO? GO WHERE?
HOMURA-CHAN IS FIGHTING.

WAIT, "FIGHTING"?
HOMURA IS? SHE'S FIGHTING THOSE MONSTERS?

SORRY!
MA-DOKA-SAN!
TA (TMP)

BITAN (SLAMMM)
GA (GRAB)
MA-DOKA-SAN!?

S...
...SAYAKA-CHAN, THAT HURT!

MADOKA, WHAT ARE YOU PLAN-NING TO DO WHEN YOU GET THERE?

I HAVE NO IDEA WHY HOMURA IS OUT THERE FIGHTING, BUT...

THAT'S WHY...
..."SAYAKA-SAN" IS GOING IN AS BACKUP.

...YOU CAN'T DO A THING TO HELP, RIGHT, MADOKA?
URK...

YOU'D END UP GETTING IN HER WAY.
SAYAKA-SAN, YOU'RE BEING TOO HARSH!

WE'RE FRIENDS, RIGHT?
I CAN'T JUST LET HER BE.
SAYAKA-SAN...

OKAY, LET'S GET MOVING! YOU TOO, HITOMI!
R-RIGHT!
NOW THAT IT'S COME TO IT, I SAY WE TAKE ON WHATEVER THEY CAN TOSS AT US!

I HAVE FOUGHT TO SAVE MITAKIHARA... TO SAVE THE ENTIRE WORLD.
BUT YOU GIRLS ...
AND YOU...

MADOKA KANAME IS GOING TO BECOME THE WORST WITCH THE WORLD HAS EVER KNOWN!
I REFUSE TO LET HER LIVE!
MADOKA WILL NEVER BECOME A MAGICAL GIRL!
I WILL SEE TO THAT.
ALSO... THERE'S SOMETHING I WANT TO ASK YOU!
BA (WHOOSH)

BARARA (SCATTER)
STOP THAT! YOUR SOUL GEM IS ALREADY AT ITS LIMIT, RIGHT!?
—!
GOPU (BLRP)
I KNOW! I KNOW THAT MADOKA KANAME WILL BE HERE VERY SOON!
I CAN'T RETREAT NOW!!
I'LL MAKE HOMURA AKEMI STOP TIME AGAIN AND AGAIN, WEAKENING HER MAGIC!
AND KIRIKA'S SPEED-SLOWING MAGIC IS STILL GOING!
DO
DO
DO
DO (BAM)
DO

AND IF HOMURA AKEMI'S TIME-STOP MAGIC IS GONE, NOTHING CAN STOP ME!
I CAN UNLEASH A FULL-POWER MAGICAL ATTACK AT THE VERY MOMENT MADOKA KANAME ENTERS!
I WILL WIN!
GYUAA (VWWWM)
DON (THOOM)
NGH!
GO (WHAM)

HYAAA!
BUN (WHSH)
TO (THUMP)
YOU LITTLE ...
HYU (WHOOSH)
YOU THINK I'M GOING TO LET YOU ATTACK !!?

HYUPA
(SLICE)
SH
(SLIP)

THAT IS NOTHING MORE THAN A CORPSE NOW.
ブアッ
BUA (VWOO)
A WISH ...?
YEP!
YOUR WISH WILL GIVE BIRTH TO A SOUL GEM!

MY...
MY WISH...
"I WANT TO HELP THE WORLD... TO HELP MY FATHER... TO HELP EVERY-BODY!
"SO I'M GOING TO WORK REALLY HARD!"
"HISAOMI MIKUNI WAS FOUND HANGED BY THE NECK IN HIS HOME."
"SHE'S A STAIN ON THE NAME OF THE SCHOOL!"
"DON'T COME HERE ANYMORE! YOU MAKE EVERY-BODY'S LIFE HARDER!"
"MIKUNI? OH, THE DAUGHTER OF THAT DIRTY POLITICIAN."
"SHE'S STILL LIVING IN OUR NEIGHBOR-HOOD! CAN YOU STAND IT?"
NO ONE SAW ME BUT THROUGH THE LENS MADE BY MY FATHER'S ACTIONS.

SO IF I'M NOTHING BUT AN EXTENSION OF MY FATHER...
...WHAT AM I LIVING FOR?
I WISH FOR...
...A REASON FOR ME TO LIVE.

DOSH (STAB)

WHAT!?

GUH... UNH...

UHHN...

I... CAN'T... LET MYSELF FALL YET...!
KARAN (KLANG)
JAKON (KACHIK)

AREN'T YOU GOING TO SHOOT?
YES, I AM!
ANSWER ONE QUES-TION.
WHY ARE YOU SO HELL-BENT ON FIGHTING?
IT'S... TO SAVE MY WORLD.
GAN (BLAM)

PAAN (BLAM)
THE WORLD WILL END VERY SOON.
HOMURA AKEMI WILL FAIL.
AND I...
...WAS UNABLE TO DO ANY-THING ABOUT IT.
PARA (CRUMBLE)

PAKIN (CRACK)
IT BREAKS MY HEART...
!
A FRAG-MENT OF KIRIKA ...?
ONE LAST...

...ATTACK!!
GAHYU (KAVOOM)
HYUO (VWOOSH)
GOU (WHOOSH)

DOSU (SLAM)
FURA (WOBBLE)
DO (WHUD)
IS IT OVER?
YES. SHE'S DEAD.

PAAAAAN
(CRUMMMBLE)

YAAAY! THE WITCH'S WARDS ARE VANISH-ING!
THAT'S ONE LESS THING TO WORRY ABOUT.

EVERY-ONE...
...THERE IS SOME-THING I THINK YOU SHOULD KNOW.

KYAAAAAA!

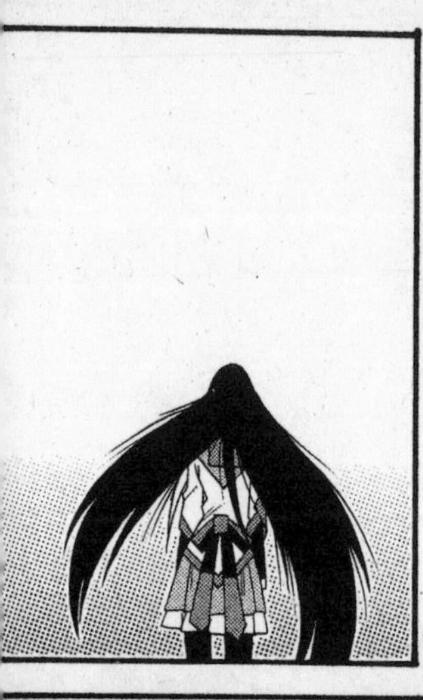

HMM?
WHAT'S ALL THE FUSS NOW?

THAT VOICE...
AH, LOOK OVER THERE! THERE'S A GIRL DOWN!

OF ALL THE LUCK!
ORIKO REALLY MESSED UP MY PLAN.

YUMA, DID YOU GET THERE IN TIME?

IT TURNS OUT ORIKO WASN'T AIMING AT ME AT ALL...
SHE WAS JUST BEYOND THE WALL.

THAT GIRL.
MADOKAAAA!!

IT'S...TO SAVE MY WORLD.
MA-DOKA! MA-DOKA!
MA-DOKA-SAN!
ANSWER ME!
WAAA-AAAH!
KACHIN (KACHINK)

Authorities have received numerous reports of the disappearances of several students and teachers from Mitakihara Middle School...
The police are investigating the incident from multiple angles—both as an accident or as a possible criminal case. However the investigation seems to be stalled because of a lack of evidence.

And now for the weather...

WHAT IS THIS? WHY ISN'T THERE ANYBODY HERE?

IS TODAY A DAY OFF OR SOMETHING?

HMM?

WHAT'S WRONG WITH YOU? WHY ARE YOU SITTING THERE?

YOU'RE NOT A STUDENT AT MY SCHOOL, I DON'T THINK.

I HAVE KILLED MANY, MANY PEOPLE.

AS A RESULT, MANY MORE PEOPLE WERE SAVED...
...BUT THE BURDEN IS STILL SO HEAVY...
...I CAN'T STAND UP.

HMM. I DON'T GET THAT, BUT...
...YOU'RE SAYING YOU'VE GOT SOME HEAVY BAGGAGE, RIGHT?

HMM...

OKAY!

HOW ABOUT I LIFT HALF OF IT FOR YOU?

EH ...?

WHAT I'M SAYING IS...

...LET'S GO TOGETHER!

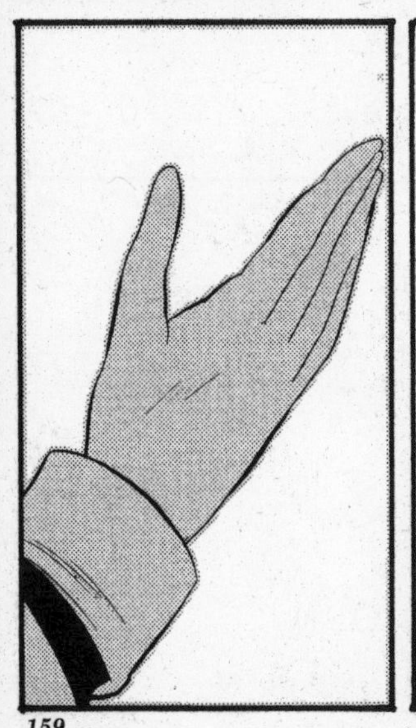